Monkeys Around

Craig Wright

Name _____

Age _____

Class _____

OXFORD
UNIVERSITY PRESS

OXFORD
UNIVERSITY PRESS

Great Clarendon Street, Oxford OX2 6DP

Oxford University Press is a department of the University of Oxford.
It furthers the University's objective of excellence in research, scholarship,
and education by publishing worldwide in

Oxford New York

Auckland Bangkok Buenos Aires Cape Town Chennai
Dar es Salaam Delhi Hong Kong Istanbul Karachi Kolkata
Kuala Lumpur Madrid Melbourne Mexico City Mumbai
Nairobi São Paulo Shanghai Taipei Tokyo Toronto

OXFORD and OXFORD ENGLISH are registered trade marks of
Oxford University Press in the UK and in certain other countries

ISBN 0 19 440077 8

Printed in Hong Kong

Illustrations by: Jan McCafferty

With thanks to Sally Spray for her contribution to this series

To Vaughan and family

Reading Dolphins
Notes for teachers & parents

📖 Using the book

1 Begin by looking at the first story page (page 2). Look at the picture and ask questions about it. Then read the story text under the picture with your students. Use section 1 of the CD for this if possible.

2 Teach and check the understanding of any new vocabulary. Note that some of the words are in the **Picture Dictionary** at the back of the book.

3 Now look at the activities on the right-hand page. Show the example to the students and instruct them to complete the activities. This may be done individually, in pairs, or as a class.

4 Do the same for the remaining pages of the book.

5 Retell the whole story more quickly, reinforcing the new vocabulary. Sections 2 and 3 of the CD can help with this.

6 If possible, listen to the expanded story (section 4 of the CD). The students should follow in their books.

7 When the book is finished, use the **Picture Dictionary** to check that students understand and remember new vocabulary. Section 5 of the CD can help with this.

💿 Using the CD

The CD contains five sections.

1 The story told slowly, with pauses. Use this during the first reading. It may also be used for "Listen and repeat" activities at any point.

2 The story told at normal speed. This should be used once the students have read the book for the first time.

3 The story chanted. Students may want to chant along with the story.

4 The expanded story. The story is told in a longer version. This will help the students understand English when it is spoken faster, as they will now know the story and the vocabulary.

5 Vocabulary. Each word in the **Picture Dictionary** is spoken and then used in a simple sentence.

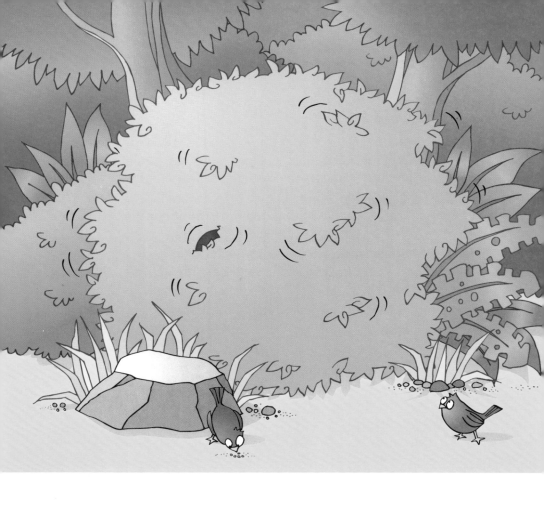

What is in the bush?

Connect.

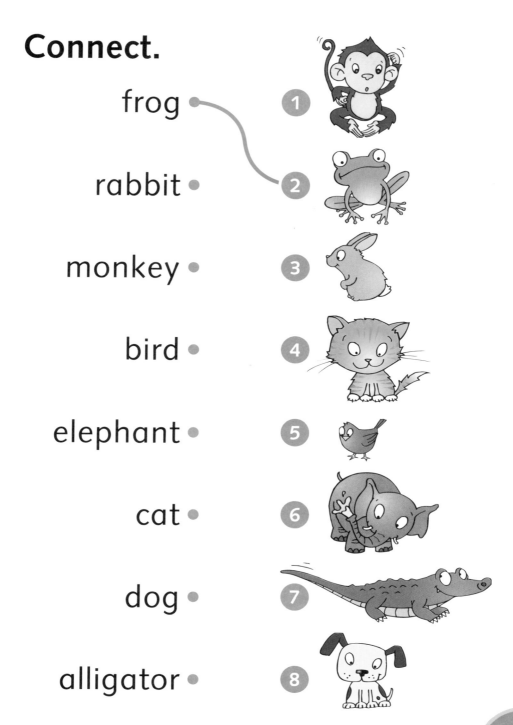

frog •

rabbit •

monkey •

bird •

elephant •

cat •

dog •

alligator •

1
2
3
4
5
6
7
8

3

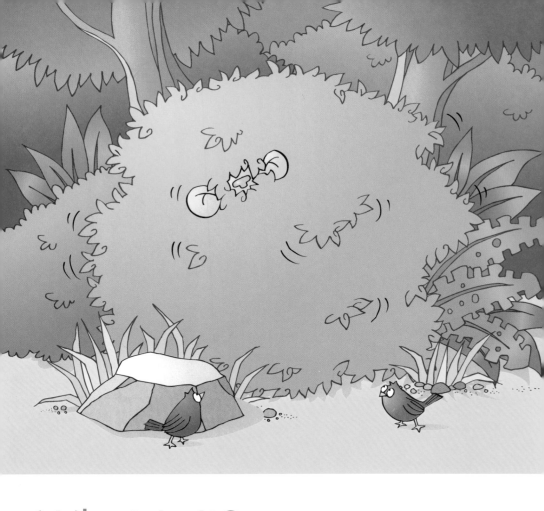

What is it?

It is a nose.

What are they?

They are ears.

Connect.

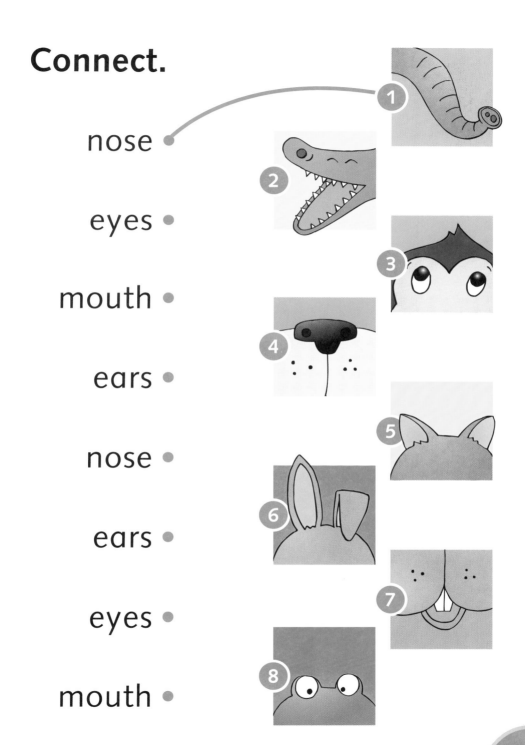

nose

eyes

mouth

ears

nose

ears

eyes

mouth

What is it?

It is a mouth.

What are they?

They are eyes.

Circle yes or no .

1 It is an eye.

2 It is an eye.
yes
no

3 It is a mouth.
yes
no

4 They are eyes.
yes
no

5 It is a mouth.
yes
no

6 It is a mouth.
yes
no

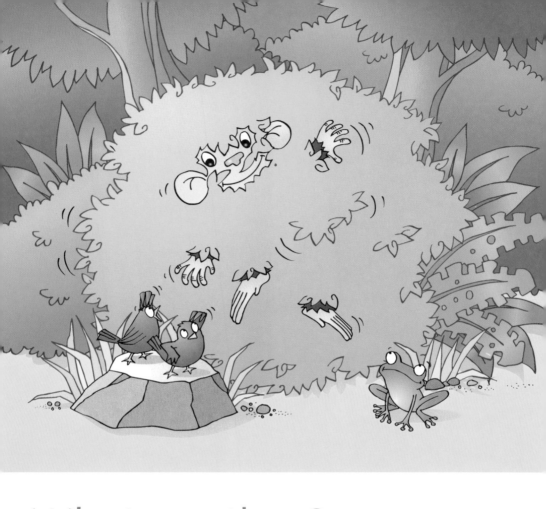

What are they?

They are hands.

What are they?

They are feet.

How many?

 6

What is it?

It is a body.

What are they?

They are legs.

Circle.

1. It is / **They are** hands.

2. It is / They are a body.

3. It is / They are ears.

4. It is / They are a nose.

5. It is / They are legs.

6. It is / They are a mouth.

What is it?

It is a tail.

What are they?

They are arms.

Circle.

1. It **is** / are a tail.

2. They is / **are** feet.

3. They is / **are** legs.

4. It **is** / are a body.

5. It **is** / are a mouth.

6. They is / **are** eyes.

13

What is it?

It is a monkey.

Number.

hand 5

body

leg

nose

tail

mouth

foot

ear

Picture Dictionary

arm

dog

bird

ear

body

elephant

cat

eye

feet

mouth

frog

nose

hand

rabbit

leg

tail

monkey

Dolphin Readers

Dolphin Readers are available at five levels, from Starter to 4.

The Dolphins series covers four major themes:

Grammar, Living Together,
The World Around Us, Science and Nature.

For each theme, there are two titles at every level.

Activity Books are available for all Dolphins.

All Dolphins are available on audio CD.
(2 TITLES ON EACH CD ⬤ SEE TABLE BELOW)

Teacher's Notes are available at **www.oup.com/elt/dolphins**

	Grammar	Living Together	The World Around Us	Science and Nature
Starter	• Silly Squirrel • Monkeying Around	• My Family • A Day with Baby	• Doctor, Doctor • Moving House	• A Game of Shapes • Baby Animals
Level 1	• Meet Molly • Where Is It?	• Little Helpers • Jack the Hero	• On Safari • Lost Kitten	• Number Magic • How's the Weather?
Level 2	• Double Trouble • Super Sam	• Candy for Breakfast • Lost!	• A Visit to the City • Matt's Mistake	• Numbers, Numbers Everywhere • Circles and Squares
Level 3	• Students in Space • What Did You Do Yesterday?	• New Girl in School • Uncle Jerry's Great Idea	• Just Like Mine • Wonderful Wild Animals	• Things That Fly • Let's Go to the Rainforest
Level 4	• The Tough Task • Yesterday, Today and Tomorrow	• We Won the Cup • Up and Down	• Where People Live • City Girl, Country Boy	• In the Ocean • Go, Gorillas, Go